YOUR KNOWLEDGE HAS VALUE

- We will publish your bachelor's and
  master's thesis, essays and papers

- Your own eBook and book -
  sold worldwide in all relevant shops

- Earn money with each sale

Upload your text at www.GRIN.com
and publish for free

Bibliographic information published by the German National Library:

The German National Library lists this publication in the National Bibliography; detailed bibliographic data are available on the Internet at http://dnb.dnb.de .

This book is copyright material and must not be copied, reproduced, transferred, distributed, leased, licensed or publicly performed or used in any way except as specifically permitted in writing by the publishers, as allowed under the terms and conditions under which it was purchased or as strictly permitted by applicable copyright law. Any unauthorized distribution or use of this text may be a direct infringement of the author s and publisher s rights and those responsible may be liable in law accordingly.

Imprint:

Copyright © 2016 GRIN Verlag
Print and binding: Books on Demand GmbH, Norderstedt Germany
ISBN: 9783668748958

This book at GRIN:

https://www.grin.com/document/432712

Jennie Robinson

The use of internet for retail investors' online share dealing and the regulatory authorities' response to the risks

GRIN Verlag

GRIN - Your knowledge has value

Since its foundation in 1998, GRIN has specialized in publishing academic texts by students, college teachers and other academics as e-book and printed book. The website www.grin.com is an ideal platform for presenting term papers, final papers, scientific essays, dissertations and specialist books.

Visit us on the internet:

http://www.grin.com/

http://www.facebook.com/grincom

http://www.twitter.com/grin_com

Introduction

The Internet is "an informal, worldwide network of computers linking millions of users", who are benefiting from new means of: "widespread and instantaneous communication, low cost, interactivity, hyperlinks, decentralization, anonymity, and flexibility"(1998 IOSCO Report)[1]. Providing financial services and selling securities have taken another level with the development of internet-based banking (1998 IOSCO Report)[2]. This assignment will address the Internet characteristics with regard to retail investors' online share dealing, and the different risks that regulatory authorities have to respond to.

Development

i. **The characteristics of the Internet and the factors that have led to widespread use of the internet for online share dealing by individual/retail investors**

Vyas defines E-banking as "a borderless entity permitting anytime, anywhere and anyhow banking". The main impact of internet banking is found on "banking relationships". Indeed, by providing mobility through the use of internet, banking services are "now no longer confined to the branches were one has to approach the branch in person, to withdraw cash or deposit a cheque or request a statement of accounts"[3]. According to Yang, with the widespread of the Internet, "electronic commerce has emerged, allowing businesses to more effectively interact with their customers and other corporations inside and outside their industries"[4]. In this context, "the typically 'non-physical' or 'dematerialized' nature of securities transactions makes the internet an appealing medium for the financial services industry". And other characteristics such as low cost, the offering of "immediacy, flexibility and interactivity" provided for "the financial services industry's ability to reach into the retail market" (1998 IOSCO Report)[5]. As such, online share dealing and execution has spread through the use of different devices such as computers, tablet, or smart phone (CeFiMS, Unit 5 – p3).[6] According to Rutlege & Haines (2007, pp.25-26), among the factors that contributed to the new reality of online trading are: "cheaper trading commissions" that are "made possible by

---

1 International Organization of Securities Commissions (1998) 'Report on Securities Activity on the Internet', Madrid: IOSCO
2 Ibid.
3 Vyas, S. 2012. 'Impact of E-Banking on Traditional Banking Services.'[online]. Available from http://arxiv.org/ftp/arxiv/papers/1209/1209.2368.pdf [accessed 27 March 2016]
4 Yang, Y. 1997. 'The security of electronic banking.'[online]. Available from http://csrc.nist.gov/nissc/1997/proceedings/041.pdf [accessed 27 March 2016]
5 International Organization of Securities Commissions (1998) 'Report on Securities Activity on the Internet', Madrid: IOSCO.
6 Center for Financial and Management Studies, 2016. Law & Regulation of Electronic Finance & Internet Banking. 3rd revision, London.

electronic automation", "free access to market information, historical data on company and share performance, and industry and analysts' reports". These factors have led millions of internet users to be "able to trade faster, cheaper and with more frequency than ever before"[7]. Another characteristic of the internet is the absence of opening hours, allowing the user, once connected, for "after-hours trading". This facility is offered by the broker-dealers for the customer to have "greater flexibility and an opportunity to manage their portfolios" (CeFiMS, Unit 5 – p.8)[8].

ii. The methods by which an order entered into on online share dealing venue is processed and executed, and the participants in that process

The "mechanical processes of online share dealing" involve three parts, which are: the front-end, the middleware, and the back-end. The front-end is the account page accessed by the investor once connecting to the broker's website. In this page, the investor is then able to access their account information and trade. The middleware leads the investor to its requested search such as "stock quotes, account information, customer support, etc.", but it also navigates the investor to "the online broker's database" and to the back-end part, which "accommodate the trading functions". The back-end part deals with the customer's trade and provides a request confirmation for the trade order passed. Upon order confirmation, "the data flows from the front-end system to the back-end system". After this step, the scrutinising of the customer takes place through "a computerized process" (from "the broker's own system" or from "a third party provider", to check for "adequate capital", for authorisation to "trade on a margin", and for other "restrictions on the customer's account" (CeFiMS, Unit 5 – p.4).[9]

Once the trade order pass a positive scrutinising process, it can be sent for "execution". Otherwise, the trade order will be "manually reviewed" by a broker's representative, and upon positive review can then be executed. The next step is the market, which consists of different type of markets such as the New York Stock Exchange in the US, an "electronic communication network (ECN)", an "over-the-counter market maker", by "internalising the order flow" through the broker acting as a "market maker", or a "clearing firm". The executed order will be notified to the online broker "directly or through the firm's back office provider

---

7   Rutlege & Haines, 2007. *Electronic Markets*, Haywards Heath UK: Tottel Publishing Ltd. Chapter 2 'Online trading: the new reality', and Chapter 5 'E-offerings: a guide to online securities offerings'.
8   Center for Financial and Management Studies, 2016. Law & Regulation of Electronic Finance & Internet Banking. 3rd revision, London.
9   Ibid.

or clearing agent", and will be accessible in the "broker's trading system" and ultimately "back to the front-end system to the customer" (CeFiMS, Unit5 – p.5).[10]

iii. The types of risks that have arisen for individual investors in regard to their use of online share dealing venues

Despite the great benefits of using internet banking, challenges and risks are also present for "securities regulators and self-regulatory organizations (SROs)". In the legal context, internet banking activity "may not fit neatly within the parameters of statutes, regulations and directives originally intended for a telephone- and paper-based environment" (1998 IOSCO Report)[11]. Security threats such as fraud or identity theft have been taking place, such as the 1995 hacking of City Bank's system, which was "the first successful penetration by a hacker into the systems that transfer trillions of dollars a day around the world's banks "(Hansell, S. 1995)[12]. Following this case, City Bank took protective measure with the use of "an electronic device that creates a new password for every transfer". And since 2013, some hackers managed to infiltrate "more than 100 banks in 30 countries" and stole "up to $1 billion", making it "unusual because they target the banks themselves rather than customers and their account information" (The Associated Press, 2015).[13] In this context, an institution such as Halifax bank in the UK reassures its customers concerning fraud: "We do all we can to protect you online. Even in the unlikely event of fraud, we promise you won't lose out. As an online share dealing customer, you automatically benefit from our online fraud guarantee", and advise customers to take steps to prevent any other security issues: by safely keeping the password and not allowing anyone to see or use the account's security, by protecting the computer against virus and updating its operating system and web browser (Hallifax Website).
[14]

According to Rutlege & Haines (2007, p.32), "both the GAO [US General Accounting Office on Online Trading] Online Report and the New York Report observed that online investors had very little appreciation of the risks and limitations posed by moving their securities trades

---

10 Ibid.
11 International Organization of Securities Commissions (1998) 'Report on Securities Activity on the Internet', Madrid: IOSCO
12 Hansell, S. 1995. 'Citibank Fraud Case Raises Computer Security Questions.' [online]. Available from http://www.nytimes.com/1995/08/19/business/citibank-fraud-case-raises-computer-security-questions.html [accessed 27 March 2016]
13 The Associated Press, 2015. 'Hacking ring steals up to $1 billion from 100 international banks: report.' [online]. Available from http://www.nydailynews.com/news/world/hacking-ring-steals-1-billion-banks-report-article-1.2116876 [accessed 27 March 2016]
14 Halifax bank, currently. 'Our fraud guarantee and online security.' [online]. Available from https://www.halifax.co.uk/sharedealing/important-information/security/ [accessed 28 March 2016]

onto an online trading system". The lack of "human representative" is felt when no one "can explain to the customer the specifics of the process and attendant risks to the transaction". And despite the benefits of online trading, investment decision-making has remained uneasy. Another risk is with the execution of a trade order, which cannot be simply done through an online click, but rather follow a certain procedure through a review market until the execution. Different factors also bring about delays in the confirmation of order executions, such as "system delays and outages", "ongoing batch process", or "pre-programmed slowdowns".[15]

According to Rutlege & Haines (2007, p.28), "outages of electronic systems used by online brokers to process trades have been the most visible problems concerning online trading encountered by individual investors". Indeed, "when the firm's website is down or inaccessible, the public investor is disadvantaged by not being able to view account details, obtain current market information or enter a trade order". These outages "were caused by problems with vendor-supplied systems, which usually handle the processing, routing or executing of orders, or were the result of systems upgrades to expand capacity or improve capacity". Due to the fact that, "each firm's systems is composed of numerous components", there is a "difficulty of assessing the adequacy of their information systems".

And thus, it has been argued that "the real issue is whether the system can accommodate peak demands, such as the market open and close, and particularly during time of high market volatility"[16].

The fluctuation of price is another risk influenced by the presence of markets and stocks volatility. Thus in order to "limit exposure to price fluctuation, an investor should place a limit order which specifies the maximum price at which the investor will agree to purchase the shares" (CeFiMS, Unit 5 – p.6)[17]. Other risk is related to "cheap and easy trading", which "does not equal successful trading" (CeFiMS, Unit 5 – p.6)[18].

The understanding of the risks related to "trading securities on margin" are: the possibility to "lose more funds than you deposit in the margin account", "the firm can force the sale of securities or other assets in your account(s)", "the firm can sell your securities or other assets without contacting you", "your are not entitled to choose which securities or other assets in your account", "the firm can increase its 'house' maintenance margin requirements at any

---

15   Rutlege & Haines, 2007. *Electronic Markets*, Haywards Heath UK: Tottel Publishing Ltd. Chapter 2 'Online trading: the new reality', and Chapter 5 'E-offerings: a guide to online securities offerings'.
16   Ibid.
17   Center for Financial and Management Studies, 2016. Law & Regulation of Electronic Finance & Internet Banking. 3rd revision, London.
18   Ibid.

time", and "you are not entitled to an extension of time on a margin call" (Rutlege & Haines, 2007, pp.36-37)[19]. While issuing a margin call (or securities sales) is a result of the decline in securities value in the customer's account, it is used « in order to maintain the required equity in the account ». However, it could require the customer to « provide additional funds to the firm » (CeFiMS, Unit 5 – p.7).[20]

Other issues are related to after-hours trading, which are the risks of « lower liquidity, higer volatility [in price], changing prices, unlinked markets [for prices], news announcements [affecting the price], and of wider spreads [in prices]» (CeFiMS, Unit 5 – pp.8-9).[21]

iv. The regulatory authorities responses and advises to some of those investor risks

The internet "provides for instantaneous cross-border communication and interactivity, which challenge traditional notions of jurisdiction and territoriality" (1998 IOSCO Report).[22] In facing this situation, the Technical Committee of the International Organization of Securities Commissions (IOSCO) formed a Task Force, in order to "examine and provide guidance on issues relating to the impact of the Internet on securities regulation", and not overstepping on the role of domestic jurisdictions to "provide legal interpretations or set universal standards". The main securities regulation were aimed at protecting investors, making sure that "securities markets are fair, efficient and transparent", and reducing "systemic risk". Among the principles to accompany regulators' policies is for instance to "strive for transparency and consistency regarding how their regulations apply in an Internet environment" (1998 IOSCO Report). While key recommendations in the "application of domestic regulatory requirements to securities activities on the internet" are among others, for the regulators to (1998 IOSCO Report)[23] :

- "provide guidance to alert market participants and markets as to how their existing registration, licensing and other regulatory requirements apply to offers and advertisements conducted on the Internet"
- "have the relevant authorities or legislative bodies amend, specific requirements when appropriate to accommodate and ensure appropriate regulatory coverage of the

---

19 Rutlege & Haines, 2007. *Electronic Markets*, Haywards Heath UK: Tottel Publishing Ltd. Chapter 2 'Online trading: the new reality', and Chapter 5 'E-offerings: a guide to online securities offerings'.
20 Center for Financial and Management Studies, 2016. Law & Regulation of Electronic Finance & Internet Banking. 3rd revision, London.
21 Ibid.
22 International Organization of Securities Commissions (1998) 'Report on Securities Activity on the Internet', Madrid: IOSCO.
23 Ibid.

Internet environment"

- deal with fraud with "general antifraud provisions" to "apply to all offers and advertisements involving securities or financial services"
- "strengthen surveillance of Internet advertising and offerings for unauthorized or fraudulent activities" (1998 IOSCO Report).[24]

Moreover, according to Rutlege & Haines (2007, p.29), the US Securities and Exchange Commission (SEC), in its 2001 Online Broker Report, suggests that firms should review their "operational capacity" by for instance: evaluating their phone capacity, their backup systems, the adequate number of phone representatives during outages and busy days, by "providing alternative means to place orders when Internet access is slow or unavailable".[25] In addition, this evaluation should lead to the development of "procedures for handling systems capacity problems" (CeFiMS, Unit 5 – p.7).26 In this context, the IOSCO Report (2003, p.17) lists different issues that firms should consider and ensure their system would provide: confidentiality, integrity, availability, authentication, and non-repudiation and accountability.27

With regards to margin calls, in 2001, the SEC gave its accord to new regulation for the NASD[28] members to deliver "mandatory margin disclosure statement to non-institutional customers", due to customer complaints showing an underestimation of "the risks of trading on margin" and misunderstanding of margin calls. The disclosure statement would include the "notification of margin calls, extensions of time for margin calls, right to dictate which security is liquidated, members raising their maintenance margin requirements" (Rutlege & Haines, 2007, pp.34-35).[29]

Another risk involved the "extended hours trading in the disclosure are of lower liquidity", "of higher volatility", "of changing prices", "of unlinked markets", "of news announcements", "of wider spreads" (Rutlege & Haines, 2007, p.38)[30]. In the United Kingdom, the "regulatory

---

24 International Organization of Securities Commissions (1998) 'Report on Securities Activity on the Internet', Madrid: IOSCO.
25 Rutlege & Haines, 2007. *Electronic Markets*, Haywards Heath UK: Tottel Publishing Ltd. Chapter 2 'Online trading: the new reality', and Chapter 5 'E-offerings: a guide to online securities offerings'.
26 Center for Financial and Management Studies, 2016. Law & Regulation of Electronic Finance & Internet Banking. 3rd revision, London.
27 International Organization of Securities Commissions (2003) 'Report on Securities Activity on the Internet III', Madrid: IOSCO.
28 The National Association of Securities Dealers (NASD) is the "self-regulatory organisation for broker-dealers in the US" (Rutlege & Haines, 2007, p.30)
29 Rutlege & Haines, 2007. *Electronic Markets*, Haywards Heath UK: Tottel Publishing Ltd. Chapter 2 'Online trading: the new reality', and Chapter 5 'E-offerings: a guide to online securities offerings'.
30 Ibid.

guidance on extended hours trading" was drawn up by the Securities and Futures Authority" (SFA). The SFA should also have brokerage firms consider issues of "customer order priority, timely execution, an aggregating orders" (SFA) (Rutlege & Haines, 2007, p.44).[31]

Conclusion

The use of Internet, as a communication tool and a vehicle of information through research or to get educational information, or for market data, has led the retail investors "to open and maintain accounts on-line and to place trading orders" (1998 IOSCO Report)[32]. As a constant flourishing place of information, the Internet has unfortunately brought fraudulent activities such as hacking data or illegal transactions, etc. Security risks continue to be challenges for regulators, industry, and jurisdictions. Indeed, "risks can be reduced but will never be eliminated" (2003 IOSCO Report, p.15).[33]

---

31 Ibid.
32 International Organization of Securities Commissions (1998) 'Report on Securities Activity on the Internet', Madrid: IOSCO.
33 International Organization of Securities Commissions (2003) 'Report on Securities Activity on the Internet III', Madrid: IOSCO.

References

Center for Financial and Management Studies, 2016. Law & Regulation of Electronic Finance & Internet Banking. 3rd revision, London.

Halifax bank, currently. 'Our fraud guarantee and online security.' [online]. Available from https://www.halifax.co.uk/sharedealing/important-information/security/ [accessed 28 March 2016]

Hansell, S. 1995. 'Citibank Fraud Case Raises Computer Security Questions.' [online]. Available from http://www.nytimes.com/1995/08/19/business/citibank-fraud-case-raises-computer-security-questions.html [accessed 27 March 2016]

International Organization of Securities Commissions (1998) 'Report on Securities Activity on the Internet', Madrid: IOSCO.

International Organization of Securities Commissions (2001) 'Report on Securities Activity on the Internet II', Madrid: IOSCO.

International Organization of Securities Commissions (2003) 'Report on Securities Activity on the Internet III', Madrid: IOSCO.

Riley & Robertson, 2014. 'FBI Said to Examine Whether Russia Tied to JPMorgan Hacking.' [online]. Available from http://www.bloomberg.com/news/articles/2014-08-27/fbi-said-to-be-probing-whether-russia-tied-to-jpmorgan-hacking [accessed 27 March 2016]
Rutlege & Haines, 2007. *Electronic Markets*, Haywards Heath UK: Tottel Publishing Ltd. Chapter 2 'Online trading: the new reality', and Chapter 5 'E-offerings: a guide to online securities offerings'.

The Associated Press, 2015. 'Hacking ring steals up to $1 billion from 100 international banks: report.' [online]. Available from http://www.nydailynews.com/news/world/hacking-ring-steals-1-billion-banks-report-article-1.2116876 [accessed 27 March 2016]

Vyas, S. 2012. 'Impact of E-Banking on Traditional Banking Services.'[online]. Available from http://arxiv.org/ftp/arxiv/papers/1209/1209.2368.pdf [accessed 27 March 2016]

Yang, Y. 1997. 'The security of electronic banking.'[online]. Available from http://csrc.nist.gov/nissc/1997/proceedings/041.pdf [accessed 27 March 2016]

YOUR KNOWLEDGE HAS VALUE

- We will publish your bachelor's and master's thesis, essays and papers

- Your own eBook and book - sold worldwide in all relevant shops

- Earn money with each sale

Upload your text at www.GRIN.com
and publish for free